Nobody
Loves You
Like Your
Parents

Nobody
Loves You
Like Your
Parents

New Leaf Press

First Printing: February 2004

Copyright © 2004 by New Leaf Press, Inc. All rights reserved. No part of this book may be reproduced in any manner whatsoever without written permission of the publisher, except in the case of brief quotations in articles and reviews. For information write: New Leaf Press, Inc., P.O. Box 726, Green Forest, AR 72638.

Cover by RSWalch Design
Interior design by Brent Spurlock
Edited by Jim Fletcher and Roger Howerton

ISBN: 0-89221-567-4
Library of Congress Catalog Card Number: 2003116020

Please visit our web site for more great titles:
www.newleafpress.net

New Leaf Press

Printed in Italy

*. . . for he hath said, I will never
leave thee, nor forsake thee.*

– Hebrews 13:5

A special gift for you

To

_____

From

_____

INTRODUCTION

I t's about relationships. How many times have you heard that? It's true, isn't it?

Life is very much tied to the relationships we have with people: family, friends, even enemies. Unless we live alone in a forest, we interact with other humans on a daily basis.

And because we are human, love becomes a huge part of our relationships. We crave it, nurture it, hope for it. For obvious reasons, those we live with are the recipients of varying degrees of love. A little one approaches because someone stepped on his finger during play-time. A phone call is about one sister needing another sister, right now. A plea from college

FATHER'S *Grace*

I vividly remember my last spanking. It was on my thirteenth birthday, as a matter of fact. Having just broken into the sophisticated ranks of the teen world, I thought I was something gives a mom or dad the opportunity to "love on" a homesick freshman.

If life is beautiful, then love is its face. The stories and vignettes in this book are about people and their relationships with those they love. They'll make you feel good, maybe make you cry, maybe cause you to think a bit more about someone who needs you.

Even the length of these love reminders have been chosen with care: sometimes you need a quick pick-me-up, a short read. Sometimes you have the time, and perhaps the need, to curl up for awhile and read about the human relationship.

Wherever you are in your life journey, take time to pause and reflect. It's all about love; everything else is just noise. Because nobody loves you like your parents.

on a stick. My father wasn't nearly as impressed as I was with my great importance and new-found independence.

I was lying on my bed. He was outside the window on a muggy October afternoon in Houston, weeding the garden. He said, "Charles come out and help me weed the garden."

I said something like: "No . . . it's my birthday, remember?" My tone was sassy and my deliberate lack of respect was eloquent. I knew better than to disobey my dad, but after all, I was the ripe old age of thirteen.

He set a new 100-meter record that autumn afternoon. He was in the house and all over me like white on rice, spanking me all the way out to the garden. As I recall, I weeded until the moonlight was shining on the pansies.

That same night, he took me out to a surprise dinner. He gave me what I deserved earlier. Later, he gave me what I did not deserve. The birthday dinner was grace. [1]

And from his fullness have we all received grace upon grace.

– John 1:16 (RSV)

I WILL *Never* LEAVE YOU

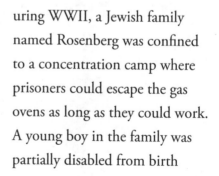

uring WWII, a Jewish family named Rosenberg was confined to a concentration camp where prisoners could escape the gas ovens as long as they could work. A young boy in the family was partially disabled from birth and could not carry a full workload. The parents were separated during the day by their separate work responsibilities, so they would hasten in the evenings to check on the condition of each family member.

One evening the father's worst fears were realized. He could not spot his disabled boy. Then he saw his older son weeping in a corner. The son told the father that the disabled boy was taken to the gas chambers because he could no longer work. The father asked, "But where is your mother?"

The older boy told how his little brother was afraid to go and clung to his mother, who said, "Don't cry. I'll go with you and hold you close." And she did. And so does Christ. Where else can you find such an inner peace as with Christ? This is the way we can run the race, never alone, but being held close to Christ.

IT'S A *Good* THOUGHT, ANYWAY

Concerned that his students were not really learning the material, an algebra teacher sent a note home to parents, asking them not to do any of the homework assigned to their children.

The next day, one student turned in a reply from his parents: "Dear Mr. Wood, we are flattered that you think we could."

After long experience in sizing up people, I definitely know you have the goods and you can go a long way. Now aren't you foolish not to get all there is out of what God has given you? . . ."

– Joseph P. Kennedy, in a letter to his 14-year-old son, John

THE SCARRED *Hands*

I read a story by Leslie Flynn who told of a small boy being raised in a frontier city by his grandmother. One night the house caught on fire. The grandmother, trying to rescue the boy who was asleep in the bedroom upstairs, was

overcome by the smoke and died in the fire. This
frontier city didn't have much of a fire department.
A crowd gathered around the house and they heard
a small boy crying out for help. The lower floor was
a wall of flames and no one seemed to know what to
do. Suddenly, a man pushed through the crowd and
began climbing an iron drainage pipe, which ran to
the roof.

The pipe was hot from the fire, but he made it to
a second floor window. The man crawled through the
window and located the boy. With the crowd cheering
encouragement, the man climbed back down the
hot iron pipe with the boy on his back and his arms
around his neck.

A few weeks later, a public meeting was held to
determine in whose custody the boy would be placed.
Each person wanting the child would be allowed to

make a brief statement. The first man said, "I have a farm and would give the boy a good home. He would grow up on the farm and learn a trade."

The second person to speak was the local schoolteacher. She said, "I am a school teacher and I would see to it that he received a good education." Finally, the banker said, "Mrs. Morton and I would be able to give the boy a fine home and a fine education. We would like him to come and live with us."

The presiding officer looked around and asked, "Is there anyone else who would like to say anything?"

From the back row, a man rose and said, "These other people may be able to offer some things I can't. All I can offer is my love." Then, he slowly removed his hands from his coat pockets. A gasp went up from the crowd because his hands were scarred terribly from climbing up and down the hot pipe. The boy

recognized the man as the one who had saved his life and ran into his waiting arms.

The farmer, teacher and the banker simply sat down. Everyone knew what the decision would be. The scarred hands proved that this man had given more than all the others.[2]

> *For ye have not received the spirit of bondage again to fear; but ye have received the Spirit of adoption, whereby we cry, Abba, Father.*
> – Romans 8:15

MY *Mother* TAUGHT ME...

y mother taught me LOGIC...
"If you fall off that swing and
break your neck, you can't go
to the store with me."

My mother taught me MEDICINE...

"If you don't stop crossing your eyes, they're going to freeze that way."

My mother taught me TO THINK AHEAD...

"If you don't pass your spelling test, you'll never get a good job!"

My mother taught me ESP...

"Put your sweater on; don't you think that I know when you're cold?"

Children, obey your parents in all things: for this is well pleasing unto the Lord.

– Colossians 3:20

Two harlots came into King Solomon's court because they had a dispute. The first woman said, "Oh my lord, I and this woman live in one house; and she was in the house when my baby was born. On the third day after my baby was born, she had her baby, and we were together. There was nobody else with us in the house — just us.

"And this woman's child died in the night; because she laid on it and smothered it. She got up at midnight, and took my son from beside me, while I was still asleep, and laid her dead child by me.

"When I got up in the morning, it was dead, but when I had thought about it, I knew it was not my son."

The other woman said, "No, the living child is my son, and the dead one is your son."

The first woman replied, "No, the dead one is yours, and the living child is my son."

Then the king said, "The one says, 'This is my son that is alive, and your son is the dead one.' And the other says, 'No, her son is the dead, and my son is the living one." So Solomon said, "Bring me a sword." And they brought a sword to him.

And the king said, "Divide the living child in two, and give half to the one, and half to the other."

Then the first woman (who was really the mother of the living child) said to the king, "Oh my lord, give her the living child, and don't kill it."

And the other said, "Let it be neither mine nor hers, but divide it."

Then the king answered and said, "Give the child to this first woman, and don't kill it. She is the real mother."

And all Israel heard of the judgment that the king had made; and they feared the king because they saw that the wisdom of God was in him, to make good judgments.

– 1 Kings 3

MIDNIGHT *Phone* CALL

Jerking up to the ringing summons, I focused on the red, illuminated numbers of my clock. Midnight. Panicky thoughts filled my sleep-dazed mind as I grabbed the receiver. "Hello?" My heart pounded, I gripped the phone

tighter and eyed my husband, who was now turning
to face my side of the bed.

"Mama?" The voice answered. I could hardly
hear the whisper over the static. But my thoughts
immediately went to my daughter. When the
desperate sound of a young crying voice became clear
on the line, I grabbed for my husband and squeezed
his wrist.

"Mama, I know it's late. But don't . . . don't say
anything until I finish. And before you ask, yes I've
been drinking. I nearly ran off the road a few miles
back and. . . ." I drew in a sharp, shallow breath,
released my husband and pressed my hand against my
forehead. Sleep still fogged my mind, and I attempted
to fight back the panic. Something wasn't right.

"And I got so scared. All I could think of was how
it would hurt you if a policeman came to your door

and said I'd been killed. I want...to come home. I know running away was wrong. I know you've been worried sick. I should have called you days ago but I was afraid . . . afraid. . . ."

Staying on the line, sobs of deep-felt emotion flowed from the receiver and poured into my heart. Immediately I pictured my daughter's face in my mind, and my fogged senses seemed to clear, "I think . . ."

"No! Please let me finish! Please!" She pleaded, not so much in anger, but in desperation. I paused and tried to think what to say. Before I could go on, she continued. "I'm pregnant, Mama. I know I shouldn't be drinking now. . . especially now, but I'm scared, Mama. So scared!"

The voice broke again, and I bit into my lip, feeling my own eyes fill with moisture. I looked up at

my husband, who sat silently mouthing, "Who is it?"

I shook my head and when I didn't answer, he jumped up and left the room, returning seconds later with a portable phone held to his ear. She must have heard the click in the line because she asked, "Are you still there? Please don't hang up on me! I need you. I feel so alone."

I clutched the phone and stared at my husband, seeking guidance. "I'm here, I wouldn't hang up, " I said.

"I should have told you, Mama. I know I should have told you. But, when we talk, you just keep telling me what I should do. You read all those pamphlets on how to talk about sex and all, but all you do is talk. You don't listen to me. You never let me tell you how I feel. It is as if my feelings aren't important. Because you're my mother you think you have all the answers. But sometimes I don't need answers. I just want someone to listen."

I swallowed the lump in my throat and stared at the how-to-talk-to-your-kids pamphlets scattered on my night stand. "I'm listening," I whispered.

"You know, back there on the road after I got the car under control, I started thinking about the baby and taking care of it. Then I saw this phone booth and it was as if I could hear you preaching to me about how people shouldn't drink and drive. So I called a taxi. I want to come home."

"That's good honey," I said, relief filling my chest. My husband came closer, sat down beside me and laced his fingers through mine.

"But you know, I think I can drive now."

"No!" I snapped. My muscles stiffened and I tightened the clasp on my husband's hand. "Please, wait for the taxi. Don't hang up on me until the taxi gets there."

"I just want to come home, Mama."

"I know. But do this for your mama. Wait for the taxi, please." Learning to listen, I listened to the silence, fearing. When I didn't hear her answer, I bit into my lip and closed my eyes. Somehow I had to stop her from driving.

"There's the taxi, now." Only when I heard someone in the background asking about a Yellow Cab did I feel my tension easing. "I'm coming home, Mama."

There was a click, and the phone went silent.

Moving from the bed, tears forming in my eyes, I walked out into the hall and went to stand in my 16-year-old daughter's room. My husband came from behind, wrapped his arms around me and rested his chin on the top of my head. I wiped the tears from my cheeks. "We have to learn to listen," I said to him.

He studied me for a second, then asked, "Do you think she'll ever know she dialed the wrong number?"

I looked at our sleeping daughter, then back at him. "Maybe it wasn't such a wrong number."

"Mom, Dad, what are you doing?" The muffled voice came from under the covers. I walked over to my daughter, who now sat up staring into the darkness.

"We're practicing," I answered.

"Practicing what?" she mumbled and lay back on the mattress, but her eyes already closed in slumber.

"Listening," I whispered and brushed a hand over her cheek.

KEEPING *Calm*

The man in the supermarket was pushing a cart which contained, among other things, a screaming baby. As the man proceeded along the aisles, he kept repeating softly, "Keep calm, George. Don't get excited, George. Don't get excited, George. Don't yell, George."

A lady watching with admiration said to the man, "You are certainly to be commended for your patience in trying to quiet little George."

"Lady," he declared, "I'm George."

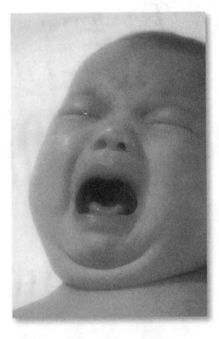

I want my children to have all the things I couldn't afford. Then I want to move in with them.

— Phyllis Diller

To the *Ends* of the Earth

T

imbuktu — the setting for a young American's strangest adventure.

For years I'd thought Timbuktu was just a made-up name for "the ends of the earth." When I found out it was a real place in Africa, I developed an inexplicable fascination for it.

It was in 1986 on a fact-finding trip to West Africa for Mission Aviation Fellowship that this fascination became an irresistible urge. Timbuktu wasn't on my itinerary, but I knew I had to go there. Once I arrived, I discovered I was in trouble. I'd hitched a ride from Bamako, Mali, 500 miles away, on the only seat left on a Navajo six-seater airplane chartered by UNICEF.

Two of their doctors were in Timbuktu and might fly back on the return flight, which meant I'd be bumped, but I decided to take the chance. Now here I was, standing by the plane on the windswept outskirts of the famous Berber outpost. There was not a spot of true green anywhere in the desolate brown Saharan landscape. Dust blew across the sky, blotting out the sun as I squinted in the 110-degree heat, trying to make out the mud-walled buildings of the village of 20,000.

The pilot approached me as I started for town. He reported that the doctors were on their way and I'd have to find another ride to Bamako.

"Try the marketplace. Someone there might have a truck, but be careful," he said, "Westerners don't last long in the desert if the truck breaks down, which often happens."

I didn't relish the thought of being stranded, but perhaps it was fitting that I should wind up like this, surrounded by the Sahara. Since I arrived in Africa the strain of the harsh environment and severe suffering of the starving peoples had left me feeling lost in a spiritual and emotional desert. The open-air marketplace in the center of town was crowded.

Men and women wore flowing robes and turbans
as protection against the sun. Most of the Berbers'
robes were dark blue, with 30 feet of material in
their turbans alone. The men were well armed with
scimitars and knives. I felt that eyes were watching me
suspiciously.

Suspicion was understandable in Timbuktu.
Nothing could be trusted here. These people had
once been prosperous and self-sufficient. Now even
their land had turned against them. Drought had
turned rich grasslands to desert. Unrelenting sun and
windstorms had nearly annihilated all animal life.
People were dying by the thousands. I went from
person to person trying to find someone who spoke
English until I finally came across a local gendarme
who understood my broken French.

"I need a truck," I said. "I need to go to Bamako." Eyes widened in his shaded face.

No truck," he shrugged. Then he added. "No road. Only sand."

By now, my presence was causing a sensation in the marketplace. I was surrounded by at least a dozen small children, jumping and dancing, begging for coins and souvenirs. The situation was extreme, I knew. I tried to think calmly. What am I to do? Suddenly I had a powerful desire to talk to my father. Certainly he had known what it was like to be a foreigner in a strange land. But my father, Nate Saint, was dead. He was one of five missionary men killed by Auca Indians in the jungles of Ecuador in 1956. I was a month shy of my fifth birthday at the time, and my memories of him were almost like movie clips, a lanky, intense man with a serious goal and a quick wit.

He was a dedicated jungle pilot, flying missionaries and medical personnel in his Piper Family Cruiser.

Even after his death, he was a presence in my life. I'd felt the need to talk with my father before, especially since I'd married and become a father myself. But in recent weeks this need had become urgent. For one thing I was new to relief work. But it was more than that. I needed Dad to help answer my new questions of faith. In Mali, for the first time in my life, I was surrounded by people who didn't share my faith, who were, in fact hostile to the Christian faith, locals and Western relief workers alike. In a way it was a parallel to the situation Dad had faced in Ecuador.

How often I'd said the same thing Dad would have said among the Indians who killed him: "My God is real. He's a personal God who lives inside me, with whom I have a very special, one-on-one relationship." And yet the question lingered in my mind: "Did my father have to die?"

All my life, people had spoken of Dad with respect; he was a man willing to die for his faith. But at the same time I couldn't help but think the murders were capricious, an accident of bad timing. Dad and his colleagues landed just as a small band of Auca men were in a bad mood for reasons that had nothing to do with faith or Americans. If Dad's plane had landed one day later, the massacre may not have happened. Couldn't there have been another way? It made little impact on the Aucas that I could see. To them it was just one more killing in a history of killings.

Thirty years later it still had an impact on me. And now, for the first time, I felt threatened because of who I was and what I believed. "God," I found myself praying as I looked around the marketplace, "I'm in trouble here. Please keep me safe and show me a way to get back. Please reveal Yourself and Your love to me the way You did to my father."

No bolt of lightning came from the blue. But a new thought did come to mind. Surely there was a telecommunications office here somewhere. I could wire Bamako to send another plane. It would be costly, but I could see no other way of getting out. "Where's the telecommunications office?" I asked another gendarme. He gave me instructions, then said, "Telegraph transmits only if station in Bamako has machine on; then message goes through. If not," he shrugged, "no answer ever comes. You only hope message received."

Now what? The sun was crossing toward the horizon. If I didn't have arrangements made by nightfall, what would happen to me? This was truly the last outpost of the world. More than a few Westerners had disappeared in the desert without a trace.

Then I remembered that just before I'd started for Timbuktu, a fellow-worker had said, "There's a famous mosque in Timbuktu. It was built from mud in the 1500's. Many Islamic pilgrims visit it every year. But there's also a tiny Christian church, which virtually no one visits. Look it up if you get the chance."

I asked the children, "Where is l'Eglise Evangelique Chretienne?" The youngsters were willing to help, though they were obviously confused about what I was looking for. Several times elderly men and women scolded them harshly as we passed, but they persisted. Finally we arrived, not at the church, but at the open doorway of a tiny mud-brick house.

No one was home, but on the wall opposite the door was a poster showing a cross covered by wounded hands. The French subscript said, "and by His stripes we are healed." Within minutes, my army of waifs pointed out a young man approaching us in the dirt alleyway. Then the children melted back into the labyrinth of the walled alleys and compounds of Timbuktu.

The young man was handsome, with dark skin and flowing robes. But there was something inexplicably different about him. His name was Nouh Ag Infa Yatara; that much I understood. Nouh signaled he knew someone who could translate for us. He led me to a compound on the edge of town where an American missionary lived. I was glad to meet the missionary, but from the moment I'd seen Nouh I'd had the feeling that we shared something in common.

"How did you come to have faith?" I asked him.

The missionary translated as Nouh answered, "This compound has always had a beautiful garden. One day when I was a small boy, a friend and I decided to steal some carrots. It was a dangerous task. We'd been told that Toubabs (white men) eat nomadic children. Despite our agility and considerable experience, I was caught by the former missionary here. Mr. Marshall didn't eat me; instead he gave me the carrots and some cards that had God's promises from the Bible written on them. He said if I learned them, he'd give me an ink pen!"

"You learned them?" I asked.

"Oh, yes! Only government men and the headmaster of the school had a Bic pen! But when

I showed off my pen at school, the teacher knew I must have spoken with a Toubab, which is strictly forbidden. He severely beat me."

When Nouh's parents found out he had portions of such a despised book defiling their house, they threw him out and forbade anyone to take him in; nor was he allowed in school. But something had happened; Nouh had come to believe that what the Bible said was true. Nouh's mother became desperate. Her own standing, as well as her family's was in jeopardy.

Finally she decided to kill her son. She obtained poison from a sorcerer and poisoned Nouh's food at a family feast. Nouh ate the food and wasn't affected. His brother, who unwittingly stole a morsel of meat from the deadly dish, became violently ill and remains partially paralyzed. Seeing God's intervention, the family and the townspeople were afraid to make further attempts on his life, but condemned him as an outcast.

After sitting a moment, I asked Nouh the question that only hours earlier I'd wanted to ask my father: "Why is your faith so important to you that you're willing to give up everything, perhaps even your life?"

"I know God loves me and I'll live with Him forever. I know it! Now I have peace where I used to be full of fear and uncertainty. Who wouldn't want to give up everything for this peace and security?"

"It couldn't have been easy for you as a teenager to take a stand that made you despised by the whole community," I said. "Where did your courage come from?"

"Mr. Marshall couldn't take me in without putting my life in jeopardy. So he gave me some books about other Christians who'd suffered for their faith. My favorite was about five young men who willingly risked their lives to take God's good news to stone age Indians in the jungles of South America."

His eyes widened. "I've lived all my life in the desert. How frightening the jungle must be! The book said these men let themselves be speared to death, even though they had guns and could have killed their attackers!"

The missionary translator said, "I remember the story. As a matter of fact, one of those men had your last name."

"Yes," I said quietly, "the pilot was my father."

"Your father?" Nouh cried. "The story is true!"

"Yes," I said, "it's true."

The missionary and Nouh and I talked through the afternoon. When they accompanied me back to the airfield that night, we found that the doctors weren't able to leave Timbuktu after all, and there was room for me on the UNICEF plane. As Nouh and I hugged each other, it seemed incredible that God loved us so much that He'd arranged for us to meet "at the ends of the earth."

Nouh and I had gifts for each other that no one else could give. I gave him the assurance that the story which had given him courage was true.

He, in turn gave me the assurance that God had used Dad's death for good. Dad, by dying, had helped give Nouh a faith worth dying for. And Nouh, in return, had helped give Dad's faith back to me. [3]

Then spake the Lord to Paul in the night by a vision, Be not afraid, but speak, and hold not thy peace: For I am with thee, and no man shall set on thee to hurt thee: For I have much people in this city.

– Acts 18:9-10

Real
ROLE MODEL

I n *Sports Spectrum*, Harold Reynolds, ESPN baseball analyst and one-time all-star second baseman for the Seattle Mariners, writes:

When I was growing up in Corvallis, Oregon, there was an NBA player named Gus Williams. Gus tied his shoes in back instead of in front like normal. I thought that was so cool. So I started tying my shoes in the back. I wanted to be like Gus. He wore number 10; I wore number 10. He wore one wristband; I wore one wristband.

One day I was lying in bed and my stomach was killing me. I noticed that it wasn't my sports hero, Gus Williams, who came to my room to take care of me.

It was my mother.

That's when I began to understand the difference between heroes and role models. I stopped looking at athletic accomplishments to determine who I wanted to pattern my life after. Instead, I tried to emulate people with strong character who were doing things of lasting value.

Whom we look up to largely determines who we become. Choose your heroes well. [4]

> *Looking unto Jesus the author and finisher of our faith;*
> *who for the joy that was set before him endured the cross,*
> *despising the shame, and is set down at the right hand of*
> *the throne of God.*
>
> – Hebrews 12:2

Finish
THE RACE

The Barcelona Olympics of 1992 provided one of track and field's most incredible moments.

Britain's Derek Redmond had dreamed all his life of winning a gold medal in the 400-meter race, and his dream was in sight as the gun sounded in the semifinals at Barcelona. He was running the race of his life and could see the finish line as he rounded the turn into the backstretch. Suddenly he felt a sharp pain go up the back of his leg. He fell face first onto the track with a torn right hamstring.

Sports Illustrated recorded the dramatic events:

As the medical attendants were approaching, Redmond fought to his feet. "It was animal instinct," he would say later. He set out hopping, in a crazed attempt to finish the race. When he reached the stretch, a large man in a T-shirt came out of the stands, hurled aside a security guard and ran to Redmond, embracing him. It was Jim Redmond, Derek's father. "You don't have to do this," he told his weeping son. "Yes, I do," said Derek. "Well, then," said Jim, "we're going to finish this together."

And they did. Fighting off security men, the son's head sometimes buried in his father's shoulder, they stayed in Derek's lane all the way to the end, as the crowd gaped, then rose and howled and wept.

Derek didn't walk away with the gold medal, but he walked away with an incredible memory of a father who, when he saw his son in pain, left his seat in the stands to help him finish the race. [5]

I have fought a good fight, I have finished my course, I have kept the faith.

– 2 Tim 4:7

MY *Mother* TAUGHT ME . . .

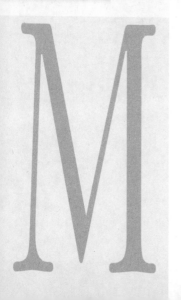

My mother taught me TO MEET A CHALLENGE...

"What were you thinking? Answer me when I talk to you...Don't talk back to me!"

My mother taught me HUMOR...

"When that lawn mower cuts off your toes, don't come running to me."

My mother taught me how to BECOME AN ADULT...

"If you don't eat your vegetables, you'll never grow up.

My mother taught me about GENETICS...

"You are just like your father!"

LETTING *Go*

avid Thomas in *Marriage and Family Living* writes:

Recently our daughter received a document of almost infinite worth to a typical fifteen year old: a learner's permit for driving.

Shortly thereafter, I accompanied her as she drove for
the first time.

In the passenger seat, having no steering wheel
and no brakes, I was, in a most explicit way, in
her hands — a strange feeling for a parent, both
disturbing and surprisingly satisfying.

As she looked to see if the road was clear, we
slowly pulled away from the curb. Meanwhile, I
checked to determine not only that, but to see if
the sky was falling or the earth quaking. If getting
from here to there was the only thing that mattered,
I would gladly have taken the wheel. But there were
other matters of importance here, most of them
having to do with my own paternal "letting go."

I experienced a strange combination of weakness
and power. My understanding of weakness was
simple: she was in control; I was not. But she was able

to move to this level of adulthood because of what my wife and I had done. Our power had empowered her. Her new-found strength was attained from us. So as we pulled away from the curb, we all gained in stature. [6]

> *I take my children everywhere, but they always find their way back home.*
>
> – Robert Orben

God's EMBROIDERY

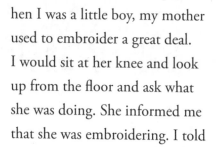

hen I was a little boy, my mother used to embroider a great deal. I would sit at her knee and look up from the floor and ask what she was doing. She informed me that she was embroidering. I told her that it looked like a mess from where I was. As from the underside I watched her work within the boundaries of the little round hoop that she held in her hand, I complained to her that it sure looked messy from where I sat.

She would smile at me, look down and gently say, "My son, you go about your playing for awhile, and when I am finished with my embroidering, I will put you on my knee and let you see it from my side."

I would wonder why she was using some dark threads along with the bright ones and why they seemed so jumbled from my view. A few minutes would pass and then I would hear Mother's voice say, "Son, come and sit on my knee." This I did only to be surprised and thrilled to see a beautiful flower or a sunset. I could not believe it, because from underneath it looked so messy.

Then Mother would say to me, "My son, from underneath it did look messy and jumbled, but you did not realize that there was a pre-drawn plan on the top. It was a design. I was only following it. Now look at it from my side and you will see what I was doing."

Many times through the years I have looked up to my Heavenly Father and said, "Father, what are You doing?"

He has answered, "I am embroidering your life."

I say, "But it looks like a mess to me. It seems so jumbled. The threads seem so dark. Why can't they all be bright?"

The Father seems to tell me, "'My child, you go about your business of doing My business, and one day I will bring you to Heaven and put you on My knee and you will see the plan from My side."

FINDING THE *Son*

L ouis Pasteur's work on viruses in human beings was interrupted by the Franco-Prussian War, which began in 1870. His only son was in the army. Earlier he had suffered the personal tragedy of losing three daughters to sicknesses. But now his son was gone to the front and weeks had passed without news. Pasteur left his laboratory and set out to find him.

The war for France was a total disaster. As Pasteur made his way north, he found the roads full of the defeated soldiers and stragglers; "the retreat from Moscow could not have been worse," he said. When he finally located his son's unit, he became even more disheartened and desperate; an officer told him that of the original twelve hundred men of the battalion, fewer than three hundred had survived.

Louis Untermeyer in *Makers of the Modern World* told of the next move by the shattered father in search of his son. "Pasteur went on through a nightmare of winding roads choked with dead horses and men suffering from freezing cold and gangrenous wounds. Finally, Pasteur recognized a gaunt soldier, weak with hunger, wrapped to his eyes in a great coat, and father and son, too moved for words, embraced in silence. [7]

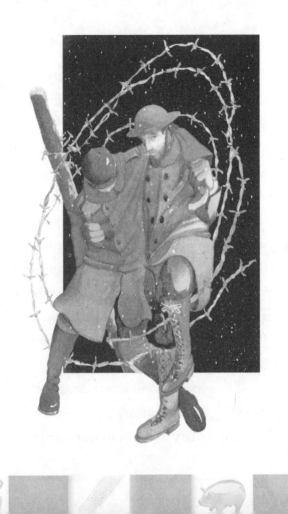

When Jesus was twelve years old, Joseph and Mary took Him and went to Jerusalem to the feast of the Passover as they did every year.

When the feast was ended, they began to return to their home, but Jesus stayed behind in Jerusalem, unknown to Joseph and Mary. Because they thought He was somewhere else in the group of travelers, they went a day's journey before they began to look for Him among their relatives and acquaintances.

When they didn't find Him, they went back to Jerusalem, looking for Him there. After three days, they found him in the temple, sitting in the midst of the teachers, learning from them, and asking questions. Everyone present was amazed at His understanding and His answers.

Joseph and Mary were astonished when they

saw Him, and Mary said, "Son, why have you done this? Your father and I were worried as we looked for you."

Jesus answered, "You should have known I would be in My Father's house."

And He went with them back home to Nazareth, and was obedient to them; and His mother pondered these events in her heart.

– from Luke 2

MY *Mother* TAUGHT ME . . .

My mother taught me about the
WISDOM of AGE...
"When you get to be my age,
you will understand."

My mother taught me about ANTICIPATION...

> "Just wait until your father gets home."

My mother taught me about RECEIVING...

> "You are going to get it when we get home."

My mother taught me to APPRECIATE A JOB
WELL DONE...

> "If you're going to kill each other, do it outside
> — I just finished cleaning!"

---

*Good advice is always certain to be ignored, but that's
no reason not to give it.*

— Agatha Christie

WHAT A *Baby* COSTS

H

ow much do babies cost?" said he
The other night upon my knee;
And then I said: "They cost a lot;
A lot of watching by a cot,
A lot of sleepless hours and care,
A lot of heartache and despair,
A lot of fear and trying dread,

And sometimes many tears are shed
In payment for our babies small,
But everyone is worth it all.

"For babies people have to pay
A heavy price from day to day —
There is no way to get on cheap.
Why, sometimes when they're fast asleep
You have to get up in the night
And go and see that they're all right.
But what they cost in constant care
And worry, does not half compare
With what they bring of joy and bliss —
You'd pay much more for just a kiss.

"Who buys a baby has to pay
A portion of the bill each day;
He has to give his time and thought
Unto the little one he's bought.
He has to stand a lot of pain
Inside his heart and not complain;
And pay with lonely days and sad
For all the happy hours he's had.
All this a baby costs, and yet
His smile is worth it all, you bet."

– Edgar Guest

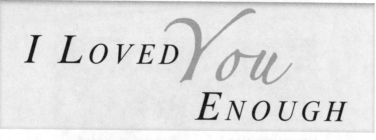

I LOVED *You* ENOUGH

Some day when my children are old enough to understand the logic that motivates a parent, I will tell them:

"I loved you enough . . . to ask where you were going, with whom, and what time you would be home."

"I loved you enough . . . to insist that you save your money and buy a bike for yourself even though we could afford to buy one for you."

"I loved you enough . . . to be silent and let you discover that your new best friend was a creep."

"I loved you enough . . . to make you take a Milky Way back to the drugstore (with a bite out of it) and tell the clerk, 'I stole this yesterday and want to pay for it.'"

"I loved you enough . . . to stand over you for two hours while you cleaned your room, a job that would have taken 15 minutes."

"I loved you enough . . . to let you see anger, disappointment and tears in my eyes. Children must learn that their parents aren't perfect."

"I loved you enough . . . to let you assume the responsibility for your actions even when the penalties were so harsh they almost broke my heart."

"But most of all, I loved you enough . . . to say no, when I knew you would hate me for it. Those were the most difficult battles of all. I'm glad I won them, because in the end you won, too."

In general my children refuse to eat anything that hasn't danced on television.

– Erma Bombeck

Mother's WISDOM

ovelist Pearl Buck told her
16-year-old daughter that she
wouldn't allow her to attend
a party of mixed teenagers
where there would be no adult
supervision.

The girl wailed, "You don't trust me!"

Mrs. Buck's reply was, "Of course I don't trust you. I couldn't trust myself at 16, 17, 18, or as much farther as you care to go! When you face the fact that you don't trust yourself in a situation, the only wisdom is to be careful not to put yourself into that situation." [8]

A mother's love for her child is like nothing else in the world. It knows no law, no pity, it dares all things and crushes down remorselessly all that stands in its path.

– Agatha Christie

MY *Mother* TAUGHT ME . . .

y mother taught me about
RELIGION...

"You better pray that will
come out of the carpet."

My mother taught me about IRONY...
  "Keep laughing and I'll give you something to cry about."

My mother taught me about CONTORTIONISM...
  "Will you just look at the dirt on the back of your neck?!"

And finally, my mother taught me about JUSTICE...
  "One day you will have kids, and I hope they turn out just like YOU. Then you'll see what it's like."

My son, hear the instruction of thy father, and forsake not the law of thy mother.
                                                    – Proverbs 1:8

PHONE *Home*

ennis Miller writes:

Out of parental concern and a desire to teach our young son responsibility, we require him to phone home when he arrives at his friend's house a few blocks away. He began to forget, however, as he grew more confident in his ability to get there without disaster befalling him.

The first time he forgot, I called to be sure he had arrived. We told him the next time it happened, he would have to come home. A few days later, however the telephone again lay silent, and I knew if he were going to learn, he would have to be punished. But I did not want to punish him! I went to the telephone, regretting that his great time would have to be spoiled by his lack of contact with his father.

As I dialed, I prayed for wisdom. "Treat him like I treat you," the Lord seemed to say. With that, as the telephone rang one time, I hung up. A few seconds later the phone rang, and it was my son.

"I'm here, Dad!"

"What took you so long to call?" I asked.

"We started playing and I forgot. But Dad, I heard the phone ring once, and I remembered."

"I'm glad you remembered," I said. "Have fun."

How often do we think of God as One who waits to punish us when we step out of line? I wonder how often He rings just once, hoping we will phone home. [9]

> *Ideal parenting is modeled after the relationship between God and man.*
>
> – James C. Dobson

Why INDEED?

parent's responsibility is not to his child's happiness; it's to his character. My father would not have been particularly interested in a book about fathering, although he did like to read.

One day when he was reading in the living room, my

brother and I decided that we could play basketball without breaking anything. When I took a shot that redesigned the glass table, my mother came in with a stick and said, "So help me, I'll bust you in half."

Without lifting his head from his book, my father said, "Why would you want twice as many?" [10]

> *Now Gideon had seventy sons, his own offspring.*
>
> – Judges 8:30 (RSV)

TIME TO *Serve*

Celine Dion once slipped behind the counter at a Florida McDonald's to serve healthy breakfasts to elementary school students, and to raise money for Ronald McDonald House (which provides housing for the families of hospitalized children). "I'm here because I'm a mother and to make a difference in my son's life is what counts the most," Dion declared. "And if I can make a difference in other children's lives, I will do it."

> *John Elway is a great football player. He used to be my son. Now I'm his father.*
>
> – Jack Elway

Because the Hebrew slaves were becoming too numerous, and he thought they might revolt and overthrow him, Pharaoh of Egypt commanded his people, "You will throw every son that is born of the Hebrews into the river, but every daughter may be allowed to live."

A Hebrew man and his wife had a son, and when she saw that he was a good child, she hid him for three months. When she could not longer hide him, she made him an ark from bulrushes, put the child in it, and placed it in the reeds in the river.

His older sister hid and watched to see what would happen.

When the daughter of Pharaoh came down to wash at the river, she saw the ark among the reeds, and she sent her maid to get it.

When she opened it, she saw the child, and the baby cried. At this, she had compassion on him and said, "This is one of the Hebrews' children."

Then the older sister said to Pharaoh's daughter, "Do you want me to go and get a nurse from the Hebrew women, so she can nurse the child for you?"

And Pharaoh's daughter said to her, "Go." And the girl went and called her own mother.

Pharaoh's daughter said to the mother, "Take this child away, and nurse it for me, and I will pay you." So the woman took the child (who was really her own), and cared for him.

When the child was ready to be weaned, she brought him to Pharaoh's daughter, and he became her son. She called his name Moses, saying, "Because I drew him out of the water."

– from Exodus 1

By faith Moses, when he was born, was hid three months of his parents, because they saw he was a proper child; and they were not afraid of the king's commandment.
– Hebrews 11:23

But *YOU GOTTA ADMIRE HIM*

n December 1950, Harry Truman's daughter, Margaret, gave a public recital in Washington. Her performance was mercilessly panned by Washington Post music critic Paul Hume, who characterized her voice as possessing "little size and fair quality" and declared that there were moments "when one can relax and feel confident that she will make her goal, which is the end of the song."

Truman, understandably incensed, promptly drafted a response:

> I have just read your lousy review buried in the back pages. You sound like a frustrated old man who never made a success, an eight-ulcer man on a four-ulcer job, and all four ulcers working.
>
> I have never met you, but if I do you'll need a new nose and plenty of beefsteak. . . .

Truman's letter was soon made public; Americans generally approved of the passion (if not the precise words) with which he came to his daughter's defense.[11]

Honored for his work with the environment, actor Harrison Ford was once invited to name a new breed of butterfly. He named it Georgia, after his daughter.

Family DIFFERENCES

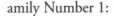

Family Number 1:

There has been careful search into the history of one criminal family known as the Jukes, and it is conspicuous as a long record of pauperism and profligacy, imbecility and insanity, prostitution and drunkenness.

A total of 1,200 descendants have been traced of this prolific family tree. Some 400 of these were physically self-wrecked, 310 professional paupers, 130 convicted criminals, 60 habitual thieves and pick-pockets, and 7 murderers; while out of the whole 1,200, only 20 ever learned a trade, and of these, half of them owed it to prison discipline.

Family Number 2:

Jonathan Edwards was the son of a godly home. His father was a preacher and before him, his mother's father. Trace the history of the offspring of this godly man.

More than 400 of them have been traced and they include 14 college presidents, and 100 professors, 100 of them have been ministers of the gospel, missionaries, and theological teachers. More than 100 of them were lawyers and judges. Out of the whole number, 60 have been doctors, and as many more, authors of high rank, or editors of journals.

In fact, almost every conspicuous American industry has had as its promoters one or more of the offspring of the Edward's stock since the remote ancestor was married in the closing half of the seventeenth century. [12]

My children are not royal; they just happen to have the Queen for their aunt.

– Princess Margaret

Kick START

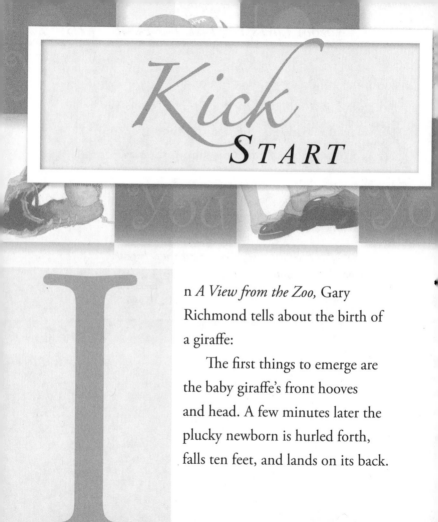

In *A View from the Zoo,* Gary Richmond tells about the birth of a giraffe:

The first things to emerge are the baby giraffe's front hooves and head. A few minutes later the plucky newborn is hurled forth, falls ten feet, and lands on its back.

Within seconds, he rolls to an upright position with his legs tucked under his body. From this position he considers the world for the first time and shakes off the last vestiges of the birthing fluid from his eyes and ears.

The mother giraffe lowers her head long enough to take a quick look. Then she positions herself directly over her calf. She waits for about a minute, and then she does the most unreasonable thing. She swings her long, pendulous leg outward and kicks her baby, so that it is sent sprawling head over heels.

When it doesn't get up, the violent process is repeated over and over again. The struggle to rise is momentous. As the baby calf grows tired, the mother kicks it again to stimulate its efforts. . . . Finally, the calf stands for the first time on its wobbly legs.

Then the mother giraffe does the most remarkable thing. She kicks it off its feet again. Why? She wants it to remember how it got up. In the wild, baby giraffes must be able to get up as quickly as possible to stay with the herd, where there is safety. Lions, hyenas, leopards, and wild hunting dogs all enjoy young giraffes, and they'd get it too, if the mother didn't teach her calf to get up quickly and get with it. . . .

I've thought about the birth of the giraffe many times. I can see its parallel in my own life. There have been many times when it seemed that I had just stood up after a trial, only to be knocked down again by the next. It was God helping me to remember how it was that I got up, urging me always to walk with Him, in His shadow, under His care. [13]

And we know that all things work together for good to
them that love God, to them who are the called according
to his purpose.

– Romans 8:28

THE MEANEST MOM IN THE WORLD

Was your mom mean? I know mine was. We had the meanest mother in the whole world! While other kids ate candy for breakfast, we had to have cereal, eggs, and toast. When others had a Pepsi and a Twinkie for lunch, we had to eat sandwiches. And you can guess our mother fixed us a dinner that was different from what other kids had, too.

Mother insisted on knowing where we were at all times. You'd think we were convicts in a prison. She had to know who our friends were, and what we were doing with them. She insisted that if we said we would be gone for an hour, we would be gone for an hour or less.

We were ashamed to admit it, but she had the nerve to break the child labor laws by making us work. We had to wash the dishes, make the beds, learn to cook, vacuum the floor, do laundry, empty the trash, and all sorts of cruel jobs. I think she would lie awake at night thinking of more things for us to do. She always insisted on us telling the truth, the whole truth, and nothing but the truth.

By the time we were teenagers, she could read our minds. Then, life was really tough! Mother wouldn't let our friends just honk the horn when they drove up. They had to come up to the door so she could meet them. While everyone else could date when they were 12 or 13, we had to wait until we were 16.

Because of our mother, we missed out on lots of things other kids experienced. None of us have ever been caught shoplifting, vandalizing others' property, or arrested for any crime. It was all her fault.

Now that we have left home, we are all educated, honest adults. We are doing our best to be mean parents just like Mom was. I think that is what's wrong with the world today. It just doesn't have enough mean moms.

THE MOST *Essential* INGREDIENT

L orne Sanny of The Navigators once wrote of his mother: "My mother gave birth to me in a frontier house on a Midwestern prairie. On the kitchen counter she placed a list of the ingredients necessary for my formula. At the top of the list was 'prayer,' and that remained at the top of her list for me throughout her life . . . I have her to thank for firmly establishing my spiritual roots." [14]

When I call to remembrance the unfeigned faith that is in thee, which dwelt first in thy grandmother Lois, and thy mother Eunice; and I am persuaded that in thee also.

– 2 Tim 1:5

I'VE *Forgotten*

n *Reader's Digest*, a contributor
told of an Aunt Ruby and Uncle
Arnie who had adopted a baby
boy after five years of trying
unsuccessfully to conceive. To their
surprise, a short time after the

adoption, Aunt Ruby discovered she was pregnant, and she later gave birth to a boy.

One day when the two boys were eight and nine years old, the teller of the story was visiting Aunt Ruby, and a woman in the neighborhood came to visit.

Observing the children at play, the woman asked, "Which boy is yours, Ruby?"

"Both of them," Aunt Ruby replied.

The caller persisted. "But I mean, which one is adopted?"

Aunt Ruby did not hesitate. In her finest hour, she looked straight at her guest and replied, "I've forgotten."

When we are adopted as God's children, we quickly come to cherish our heavenly Father's forgetfulness. For He chooses to forget our sins, to forget our wayward past, and to give us the full rights of sons or daughters. He treats us as if we had never sinned. [15]

For you did not receive the spirit of slavery to fall back into fear, but you have received the spirit of sonship. When we cry, "Abba! Father!"

– Romans 8:15 (RSV)

FATHER'S
Blessings

ary Smalley, popular author and psychologist, asked 100 people, "What is one specific way you knew that you had received your father's blessing?" Here are some of those answers:

1. "My father would put his arm around me at church and let me lay my head on his shoulder."
2. "When my father was facing being transferred at work, he purposely took another job so that I could finish my senior year in high school at the same school."
3. "When I wrecked my parents' car, my father's first reaction was to hug me and let me cry instead of yelling at me."
4. "When I was thirteen, my dad trusted me to use his favorite hunting rifle when I was invited to go hunting with a friend and his father."
5. "My father went with me when I had to take back an ugly dress a saleswoman had talked me into buying."

6. "My father would let me practice pitching to him for a long time when he got home from work."

7. "Even though I had never seen him cry before, my father cried during my wedding because he was going to miss me at home." [16]

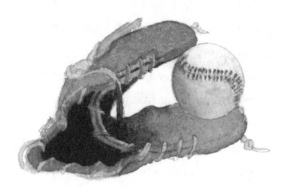

His lord said unto him, Well done, thou good and faithful servant: thou hast been faithful over a few things, I will make thee ruler over many things: enter thou into the joy of thy lord.

– Matthew 25:21

There was a man named Elkanah and his wife's name was Hannah. Because she was barren and had no children, she wept sorrowfully, and did not eat.

Elkanah said to her, "Hannah, why are you crying? Why don't you eat? Why is your heart grieved? Am I not better to you than ten sons?"

So the next time that Hannah went to the temple, she vowed a vow, and said, "Oh Lord of hosts, if you will look on the affliction of Your handmaid, and remember me, and not forget me, but will give to me a son, then I will dedicate him to You all the days of his life."

Later, Hannah did conceive, and she had a son, and called his name Samuel, saying, "Because I have asked him of the Lord."

When she had weaned him, she took him with her to the house of the Lord in Shiloh.

Then she said, "For this child I prayed; and the Lord has given me my petition which I asked of Him. Now, I will keep my vow and dedicate him to the Lord as long as he lives."

Then she prayed and said, "My heart rejoices in the Lord; my horn is exalted in the Lord; my mouth is enlarged over my enemies; because I rejoice in thy salvation."

– 1 Samuel 1:1-2:1

Whenever I held my newborn baby in my arms, I used to think that what I said and did to him could have an influence not only on him but on all whom he met, not only for a day or a month or a year, but for all eternity — a very challenging and exciting thought for a mother.

– Rose Kennedy

Never AGAIN

One Sunday I was entertained in the farm home of a member of a rural church. I was impressed by the intelligence and unusually good behavior of the only child in the home, a little four-year-old boy.

Then I discovered one reason for the child's charm. The mother was at the kitchen sink, washing the intricate parts of the cream separator when the little boy came to her with a magazine.

"Mother," he asked, "what is this man in the picture doing?" To my surprise she dried her hands, sat down on a chair and taking the boy in her lap she spent the next few minutes answering his questions.

After the child had left, I commented on her having interrupted her chores to answer the boy's question, saying, "Most mothers wouldn't have bothered."

"I expect to be washing cream separators for the rest of my life," she told me, "but never again will my son ask me that question."

I have a dream that my four little children will one day live in a nation where they will not be judged by the color of their skin but by the content of their character.

– Martin Luther King, Jr.

THE *Bridge* BUILDER

An old man, going a lone highway,
Came, at the evening, cold and gray,
To a chasm, vast, and deep, and wide,
Through which was flowing a sullen tide.
The old man crossed in the twilight dim;
The sullen stream had no fears for him;
But he turned, when safe on the
   other side,

And built a bridge to span the tide.
"Old man," said a fellow pilgrim, near,
"You are wasting strength with building here;
Your journey will end with the ending day;
You never again must pass this way;
You have crossed the chasm, deep and wide —
Why build you the bridge at the eventide?"

The builder lifted his old gray head:
"Good friend, in the path I have come," he said,
"There followeth after me today
A youth, whose feet must pass this way.
This chasm, that has been naught to me,
To that fair-haired youth may a pitfall be.
He, too, must cross in the twilight dim;
Good friend, I am building the bridge for him."

– Will Allen Dromgoole

Nothing I've ever done has given me more joys and rewards than being a father to my children.

– Bill Cosby

END NOTES

[1] Craig Brian Larson, *750 Engaging Illustrations for Preachers, Teachers, and Writers* (Grand Rapids, MI: Baker Books, 2002), p. 283, quoting from Charles Swindoll, *The Grace Awakening*, (Dallas: Word, 1990)

[2] Robert L. Allen, *His Finest Days: Ten Sermons for Holy Week and the Easter Season*, (CSS Publishing Company, 1993).

[3] Stephen Saint, Ocala, Florida, collected on the Internet

[4] Larson, *750 Engaging Illustrations for Preachers, Teachers, and Writers*, p. 615, quoting from Harold Reynolds with Roxanne Robbins, "I Couldn't Have Hand-Picked a Better Family," *Sports Spectrum*, September 1997.

[5] Wayne Rice, *Hot Illustrations for Youth Talks*

[6] Larson, *750 Engaging Illustrations for Preachers, Teachers, and Writers*, p. 150

[7] Paul Lee Tan, *Encyclopedia of 7700 Illustrations*, (Rockville, MD: Assurance Publishers), 1979, p. 963.

[8] *Homemade*, May, 1989.

[9] Larson, *750 Engaging Illustrations for Preachers, Teachers, and Writers*, p. 168.

[10] Bill Cosby, *Fatherhood*, Doubleday.

[11] F. Muir, *Irreverent Social History*

[12] Tan, *Encyclopedia of 7700 Illustrations*, p. 961-962.

[13] Craig Brian Larson, *750 Engaging Illustrations for Preachers, Teachers, and Writers*, p. 776.

[14] "Today in the Word," January, 1990, p. 23.

[15] Larson, *750 Engaging Illustrations for Preachers, Teachers, and Writers*, p. 7, quoting from "A Perfect Squelch," *Reader's Digest*, September 1990

[16] Gary Smalley, Adapted for eSermons.com, Sept 2003

Photo Credits